YORKSHIRE

Yorksher Thowts for Yorksher Folk
(and lesser breeds who want to learn summat)

Collected by Austin Mitchell
(Professional Yorkshireman)

Fowerword by Richard Whiteley
TYKONIA OMNIA VINCIT

Drawings by Stephen Abbey

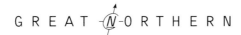

GREAT NORTHERN

GREAT NORTHERN BOOKS
P.O. Box 213, Ilkley, LS29 9WS

© Text, Austin Mitchell 2004
© Illustrations, Stephen Abbey 2004

ISBN: 1 905080 01 8

Printed by The Amadeus Press, Bradford

British Cataloguing in Publication Data:
A catalogue for this book is available from the British Library

A Word in't Lug 'Ole

Bonny Yorksher. How aw luv thi
Hard an' rugged tho' thi' face is
There's an honest air abaat thi'
Aw ne'er find i' other places
Theres a music i' thi lingo
Spreads a charm o'er 'ill an' valley
As a drop or Yorksher stingo
Arms an' cheers a body's bally

Fowerword

by Richard Whiteley, OBE, King's Cross & Bar

I met Austin Mitchell.

Richard Whiteley (V.A.T. Registered)

A good wife nivver Grumbles
WOMEN (page 61)

Yorkshire born and Yorkshire bred – strong in t'arm and thick int' 'ead
(page 64)

T' Introduction

Yorkshire is what Yorkshire sez

Na then thee.

Yorkshire's sayings are the bridge between two worlds. The first is the Yorkshire that made them, and us: the world of Methodism and mills, chapels and coal, Liberalism and Labour, and the great town halls which were declarations of UDI. The second is today's pale province. Broad Acres of chapels and mills converted to des reses or art galleries, the back-to-backs pulled down, replaced by monuments to Poulson, and the cottages and barns of the Dales filled at weekends by commuters. It's enlarged, Greater Yorkshire with new added Humberside, and to that degree diluted. One world, warm and companiable, smokey and hard, proud and independent, is fading, to be replaced by another more glossy but less difficult (i.e. bolshy) and independent (i.e. bloody) minded because more dependent on and drained by the Great Wen of London but still recognisably Yorkshire. Our Yorkshire sayings are the continuity, the main umbilical link between them.

Yorkshire is, as Yorkshire says. Which is always in short order. We are basic, direct and honest, though a little inflexible or, as Elizabeth I's Archbishop of York put it in 1580, "a more stiff-necked, wilful or abstract people did I ever know". Our sayings are just the same because they're of our essence. No need to say more, to elaborate on the obvious or go in for language so flowery Alan Tichmarsh could have written it. We're the chosen people. We don't have to justify ourselves. Particularly not to ourselves. On the other hand, our judgements on others can be as critical as we want; always reduced to the few simple phrases necessary to tell them just how inadequate they are compared to us. It is after all for their own good.

We are what we say. Us is us sayings. Us sayings is us. They are the folk wisdom of the proudest people and the most important and best part of Britain where York was a capital when London was a swamp, its writ running the Roman world before London's reached Balham. Us sayings is our literature, our weltanschauung, our philosophy and what used to be our way of life. This is the first ever collection of Yorkshire sayings. The collected wisdom of God's Own County. Over 1,500 gems of wisdom, an amazing number from such a surly, taciturn lot. After all, Yorkshirefolk are folk of few words and most of those are "bugger off". We don't say much on the basis of the old adage that life is easier that way.

> "It'll save thi no small trouble
> If when speaking you take care
> Of whom you speak to whom you speak
> And how and when and where."

Yet thanks to this cautious cannyness everything we do say is bloody good sense: mirabile dicta, as they say in Harrogate. Wise. Cryptic. Boiled down to its essence and pithily put. So here they are. Read, learn and thoroughly digest. They don't make them like this any more.

No other county, country or even continent has so much wisdom to offer: Canada, with thirty one million people, has only 1,200 sayings and a mere 135 ways of saying "stupid", all set down in Cassalman's Canadian Sayings. Yorkshire's constitute a philosophy: the people's philosophy as Tony Blair might put it. Each defines something true in the Yorkshire experience and puts it with more eloquence than a paragraph of prose or a volume of poetry. So collected together they become the collective wisdom of the wisest folk around: the product of our folk and our history handed down to us by our ancestors via parents and the benign processes of growing up in Yorkshire homes, schools and neighbourhoods. They are something proud to look back at.

As John Hartley put it: Lukkin ahead wor mi pleasure once
As aw stumbled along life's track
But nah ah've grown old me hooaps are cold
An' mi pleasure is in lukkin back

The Yorkshire phraseology may be antique - not many chapel 'at pegs around these days and few dolly pegs, while "two o'chips", an enormous quantity when fish were five pence and cakes tuppence halfpenny, would today be two chips and some scraps at two quid a packet. Yorkshire kids were called "clatter clogs long after they'd ceased to wear them (though I did - for a whole week), yet the perceptions and the sayings are eternal, an accumulated wisdom. Which is why it is important to set them down before the wisdom of generations of humanity's finest flowering is relegated to old people's homes, diluted to a meaningless mumble or driven out by the products of TV scriptwriters, political spin doctors, Clever Dick phrase-makers and the inrushing tide of globalisation and Americanisation. In France the Academie Francais would fight a bitter rearguard action. Here the Yorkshire Studies Department of York University isn't up to that job. So it has to be People Power as Yorkshire speyks to the world in its own language and lesser breeds without the county read, learn and thoroughly digest. It'll do them good.

Us sayings are as much part of Yorkshire as Ingleborough and Heckmondwike. They are our folk memory: thoughts handed down from, and by, previous generations. I learned many of them as they were used by my mother. She in turn had heard them from her mother, making us both part of that vast collection of sayings sedimented - or filed - in the Yorkshire psyche and in mum's brain. Like jokes in Ken Dodd's. Mum had a platitude for every occasion, a saying for every problem, though usually of the "Little birds in their nests agree" type as my brother and I slugged it out. She'd have made a marvellous Blairite Prime Minister, though unfortunately she lived in a time when Prime Ministers were expected to do something, not just platitudinise about it.

None of mum's sayings were dirty but many real ones are. She came from genteel, non-conformist Halifax. Some of her repertoire was pure traditional Yorkshire. Some was drawn from the rising tide of catch phrases which began to drive out traditional sayings as it poured out of the radio. Some was folk wisdom used all over the country. All this came together to linger in the collective subconscious and hers. Sadly, now the transmission mechanism is breaking down and oddly, for no reason I can understand, Yorkshire inventiveness isn't adding to the accumulated folk wisdom. It should. Churchill's adage about Jaw Jaw being better than war is better put in Tyke talk as Kall not Kill. "Gobshyte" is vivid for spoken rubbish but "Computershyte", far better than "Spam", hasn't emerged. The most recent cryptic comments I found have been "his toast dun't pop up" (pre-Viagra, of course). Yet this lack is almost certainly due to the absence of a modern Yorkshire transmission system of the type the almanacs provided rather than a weakening of Yorkshire inventiveness. Seth Armstrong of Emmerdale became the modern equivalent of the almanacs and on TV as well. Sadly he can't tell 'em like Hartley and what he says doesn't rhyme.

I bitterly regret that I failed to hand this folk wisdom on to my kids. My wife, whose job it should really be, is a Kiwi. She's given them a wholly different set of sayings: "box o' birds" when she's chirpy, "up at sparrow fart" when she's early, "flash" when they're smart, other things Yorkshire kids shouldn't be told. I'm not alone. A whole generation has failed to hand our wisdom on to its kids. No wonder today's youngsters are intellectually deprived. They grow up with politically correct circumlocutions like "visually assaulted" where once we'd say "looking like the back end of a bus", "an interesting exchange of views" rather than "a load of backslavver". Today's generation don't use these sayings automatically because they're not programmed to them as I was by growing up with them. Which makes it time to ensure that Yorkshire's great sayings don't die out so life won't lose its colour, philosophy its consolations, psychology its counsellor. So this is my attempt to atone for that failure to communicate Yorkshire's legacy to my own children; indeed, my failure to be with them enough to do so by setting them down in all their splendour so that future generations, like my grandchildren, don't lose them. They'll be the poorer for it if they do. So it's time to ensure that today's Young Yorkshire and our progency born outside the Broad Acres has them available. Then they'll use them and give a new lease of life to what should and will be eternal.

Thanks Mum. I hear you saying these verities now. I wish I'd written them down at the time but I couldn't follow you with pencil and pad, you might have asked me to do some housework or go out for "a cake and two". But perhaps there was no need because they keep coming back like a song. Mum's sayings are the core of this book, joined now by many others heard or contributed from all over the civilised world and even outside Yorkshire. Some have a definite date of origin having come from the outpourings of that great Yorkshire folk philosopher, John Hartley, with his unique ability to coin both good advice and sage observation in phrases and sayings which in turn became part of the folk legacy. A smaller number of sayings come from the other folk poets or almanac writers, like Ben Preston. Others are drawn from that great repository of Yorkshire folk lore, wisdom and wit, the Dalesman, particularly from its vintage years, the Sixties and Seventies, before, like Yorkshire itself, it became less folksy. Yet Old Amos still continues, though largely de-Yorkshified, and for those who don't see the Dalesman, Richard Whiteley could be the modern Amos. If he ever ages enough. The Dales, which once rang with the Celtic (pre-Yorkshire) sheep count of "tang-the Yan, tean tethera methera, pimp", now know only the one hundred, two hundred, three hundred, four hundred, five hundred thousand count of escalating property values. Brass blandises.

In today's world the flow of sayings has been reversed. It no longer comes from the people upwards but from the media downwards. Some of this new outpouring is popular sayings re-written by clever writers with an ear for the people, more of it is invented. Some lingers and becomes re-naturalised. Most is too ephemeral and fades quickly away. Yet all are downpourings not uprisings, a manufactured philosophy not the product of hard lives and sad experiences. Yorkshire sayings are the product of Yorkshire life but media catchphrases are the outpourings of a machine intended for a universal, not a particular, audience.

Richard Blakeborough wrote in his great book (indeed enormous because it included the wit of Yorkshire) published in 1898 that Yorkshire was a language not a dialect. In the last century it became a dialect, ending as an accent, hard and honest, and a set of sayings which are the same. So before Yorkshire - yes, even Yorkshire - can be blandised into some great blancmange of "Englishness" (which is what we're not) humanity's finest flowering must assert and blazen its uniqueness, its way of thinking, its folk memory, its folk philosophy. Yorkshire's sayings all need to be preserved because they're the essence of Us, the language of real people and the philosophy of Britain's best.

Parental Guidance Required. Some of these sayings might shock Alistair Campbell. They're not for the Southerners or the squeamish. They are the language real people talk and the things that interest them: sex and its processes, home, work, shit and its production and disposal. Yet they are all words for the wise, and all about us. Women, particularly their acidified version, feminists, may be doubtful about a few of the sayings. Yet their organised sexual sourness has had a weaker impact on paternalistic Yorkshire people than elsewhere. So most Yorkshire women will welcome it, just as they still do the occasional friendly pat on the bottom (not a reportable offence yet in Yorkshire). They recognise that their sex has a special warm place reserved for them in Yorkshire. It's called a scullery. Yorkshire women have been happy there in a way later generations and women elsewhere haven't been because they've lost sight of the simple virtues set out here. Yorkshire women recognise that the scullery is their control room. They run the world from there and reduce everything to their common sense perspective. David Hockney met his mother coming from Bradford at Los Angeles airport one Monday morning. He drove her round Los Angeles in his big limo to show her the huge houses, manicured lawns, lavish pools and trees. "How do you like that, mum?" "Well, it's all right, I suppose. But where's all t'washing?"

Yorkshire folk are what they say. Misanthropic (as they say in Harrogate), gruff, cryptic and modest. We never play owt up. We're always "fair to middlin'" never bouncing like a budgie on Trill. We're mean: when a Yorkshireman was killed picking a penny up out of the road the verdict was "death by natural causes". We're always "managing" never coining brass hand over fist. Your Tyke "meks a bob or two". Never a fortune. This isn't false modesty. T.S. Elliot got it wrong when he wrote about assurance sitting "like the silk hat on a Bradford millionaire", it's a natural contentment coupled with an obsessive secrecy, a desire to give nowt away. Mind your own business is the maxim he lives by and he knows that another Yorkshireman wouldn't ask and anyone else has no right to know. Yet he's also modest, content to be a Yorkshireman, which is enough for anyone, and never boastful unless about the beauties of Yorkshire.

Our sayings sum us up. They are us: of us, by us, for us. Not exactly generous, except with our advice for, and judgements on, other people, for there's no fault devoid of explanation. Shrewdly perceptive about faults, particularly those of others - witness the long sections on daftness, stupidity and other afflictions, right up to death. For we're a bit morbid but we're also self-sufficient, hard-working, diligent and honest. Never above making a bob or two on the side, of course that's what life's about. Above all, remember that the lesson from our sayings is that you can't fool us Yorkshire folk. We've got brilliant, built-in, fault finding and shit detection systems. Who was it vowed "We won't be fooled again?" Tykes won't be fooled the first time.

Yorkshire folk, like Yorkshire sayings, are the products of our industrial society. Life was hard, brass short, fun scarce. Yet struggle gives a shrewd perception of human weaknesses as well as a discipline and a sense of duty. Inevitably, therefore, the sections on faults, stupidity, incompetence and simple idiocy are as large as they are necessary. In those days every village had its idiot who needed neither vocational guidance nor an NVQ for the job. Villages had their cripples, the walking wounded of war and industry, their boozers and their deadbeats, and none were figures of fun. Just a feeling of "there but for the grace of God" and a warm support. After all there's a lot more daftness and a lot more faults outside Yorkshire than in it.

The reverse of this shrewdness is our pride in the county, its Broad Acres, and its inhabitants, i.e. us, though we're not exactly flowing with consolation for others without our advantages. Yorkshire folk are not naturally warm and sympathetic. Tea and sympathy are available (for a fee). But you'd do better paying for a psychiatrist or some other prostitute than coming to Yorkshire. All you'll get from us is a sharp delineation of your problems and prospects. Which will be helpful. But won't cheer you up. Hear what comfortable words our Saviour sayeth by all means, but remember, He's not from Yorkshire. Only his Father.

Us legacy is now threatened. Elocution teachers have tried in vain to stamp out the language but television and the London media blandise, political correctness drives out colour and any mention of it. Yorkshire folk go south for work and a living and can't call a spade a spade, or anything but an optimised earth-moving hand tool, the internet offers no automatic translation or Tyke search engines and the Broad Acres are now broader as Greater Yorkshire - God's own region not county. It's a matter of duty to preserve the legacy, organise it and offer its full richness to the next generation. That will break the myth that it's Grim up North. It's not, it's colourful, vivid and better expressed than owt else.

Even worse, our uniqueness is under threat. The basic industries which shaped our way of life and gave us so much of our vocabulary and sayings shrink and fade as coal, steel, fishing and wool decline, communities and chimneys are pulled down, the great consumer society takes over and national media deluge and hose us down with alien cultures: London, Birmingham, Scotland and other lesser breeds without the county. So the saying production line slows and the colour and vividness of the product fades. It's not that they don't make them like this any more. But they don't make them this Yorkshire. Many of us like living in the past - life's cheaper that way - but not so many of us now speak it. Yorkshire had led the world in the production of Yorkshire phrases as well as wool and ours were the most graphic and colourful. In the twentieth century the production line broke. John Hartley died. Comedians went south and most TV soaps are about obnoxious folk so daft they live in the East End or Salford.

Yorkshire's accumulated folk wisdom must be preserved in its own right. Still living, no collection can be complete. This is the work of one geriatric approaching senility who can't know it all, even if he's a Yorkshireman. Please help to add to the stock by telling us anything that's been missed for the next edition. Or indeed anything that's new, funny or worth preserving. Drop us a line or an email to the address on page 2. No C.O.D., of course. I'm a Yorkshireman after all. And don't be a dialect purist. My spellings and t't't' tutting aren't always consistant. But then I am a politician.

Incomplete though this first attempt at collecting Yorkshire's wit and wisdom may be, all can still benefit from it, women and outsiders more than Yorkshire men, but everyone concerned by the frivolity and shallowness of our modern world should heed it. The antidote to today's follies and fashions is the distilled, eternal, wisdom of the wisest folk on earth. That wisdom shaped our thinking and made us what we are today. Though purists flinch and philosophers sneer, we'll keep the sayings flowing here and those who ignore them do so at their peril. As the Keighley Kid, Alistair Campbell, might put it, they can go forth and multiply. Hopefully after buying the book. The rest of us can read, learn and inwardly digest, and use the sayings to awe and baffle folk outside Yorkshire. Enjoy. If tha dun't want thumping. But most of all be proud to bi Yorksher.

> "Ah's open gobbed an' soft like
> Ah know more than ah tell
> The fella that wud bite me
> Will safe get bit hi'sel
> Ah's Yorkshire"

ANGER
Ah'll 'ave thi guts for garters

Yorkshire Sayings

Abuse

Did your mother have any children that lived?

Like a clown at a funeral

When tha wants to play I'll forget t'refine

The village is missing its idiot

Anger

She's a temper in search of a tantrum

Ah'm that mad I could spit rust

A face as black as t'fire back

Ah'll 'ave thi guts for garters

Appearance

Sparrer shanks [thin legs]

Dressed like t'dog's dinner

A reet lad-lass

Nivver judge a blade by t'heft [handle]

Dressed up like two o'chips

Looking all roads for Sunday [cross-eyed]

As fat as a mawk [maggot]

She's like a bag o' bones

Ah'll drink thi beautiful

She's a face to stop a clock

So bald have seen better

Awkward

Thi mam wants thi booits for loaf tins

Tha's worse ner a dog in a snicket

Ee's more taps ner nails

Tha frames nobbut badly

Tha's a reet clatterclogs

Blabber mouth

Tha jars mi earole

Tha could 'av knocked mi down wi' a foot o' sliver

13

A big tawker int a deep thinker

'Im as boasts he allus speyks 'is
mind wudn't 'av much ter say if
ee spoke nowt else

A gob as wide as t'Umber

Bellin an' bawlin'

She's allus sticking 'er fillings in

Ee babbles like Bradford beck

Tha knows some clog iron

A reet blatherskyte

Tha's full o'blackslavver

A reet slaver-bab

Nowt but a slobbergob

That's braidin it

She's allus kallin

More gob n'er brain

She'll gie thi some gob

Ee goes round bi Leeds an' Otley

She'd tawk t'ears off a donkey

She'll tawk yer 'ead off

Ee runs off at t'mouth like a
soup sandwich

Ask him t'time o' day and he'll
tell yer how to mek a watch

Empty vessels make t'most noise

Ee's full o' clog iron and twice
as noisy

Booze

Tha's a soss pot
[sometimes a 'reet soss pot']

A deal o' t'owd age pensions goes
to support young publicans

A few jars wean't harm if tha
dun't ower do it

Talk's cheap, but it teks money
to buy whisky

Drunken men and childer speak
the truth

Drink in, wits out

As drunk as a wheel head / a
sweep / a fuzzock [= donkey] / a
newt / a skunk

Drink's like a sack-tackle. It lifts
a chap up to start wi but brings im
dahn at t'finish. *John Hartley*

Tha can't preserve dignity in alcohol

Drinken ter drown yor sorrow is like
cutting off yer tooa ter cure a corn

BOOZE

A few jars wean't harm if tha dun't ower do it

Ale weant work an' it weant laike
quietly awther

It's a poor belly 'at can't warm a
drop of ale

As dry as a lime-burner's clogs

Oft tha's made me friends mi foos
Oft tha's made me pop me cloas
But noa that thas so near me mose
Up tha comes an down tha goas

It's t'drink talking

Tha's an owd ale cart

A stuttering king and a druffen
queen [How the Misses
Murgatroyd next door used
to describe George VI]

As pissed as a newt
And don't forget the gentle cries
of closing time: "Sup up an'
gerrome", "T' rag's up", or, in the
occasional upmarket hostelry,
"You hav been here too long for
any good that you are doing. Be
gone and let us have done with
you. In the name of God go."

Boredom

There's so little to do i'
Eckmondwikewe 'ad t'watch
t'Co-op bacon slicer

Miserable as a week o' wet
Wednesdays

For summat lively we'd watch
t'traffic lights change

We used to go to t'graveyard for
a bit of excitement

It wor almost as slow as
rigor mortis

Dead boring like necrophilia

Brass

It's capping sometimes what a
ha'pence can do

A chap at doesn't care for brass
may be goin to t'dogs
But a chap at cares for nowt but
brass has gitten theer. *John
Hartley*
If tha want to lose a pal, lend 'im
some brass
It's true at brass keeps goin' rahnd
An' noon but fouls would try to
stop it
But what a chap would like t'know
Is hah to chase it rahnd an' cop it.
Walter Hampson

Ee chucks 'is brass around like a
man wi no arms

When we say money is the root
of all evil we mean other fowk's
money not ours

Th' more brass a man gets an' th'
more stuff ee puts in 'is belly –

an' the more a woman gets the
more she puts on her back

Brass burns a hole in his pocket

Aye it's grand to ha' plenty o' brass
John Hartley

If tha Bob dunt gee our Bob t'bob
as thi Bob owes our Bob our Bob
'll gie thi Bob a bob on't nose

Love of brass is t'root of half
t'world's troubles an' lack of it
t'root of t'other 'alf

Na then Bradford. 'Ow are yer?

Don't forget the diver sir. Don't
forget the diver

Titter ye not at the afflicted

Trouble at t'mill

Are yer courtin'?

TTFN – Ta Ta for Now

Get that effin ferret off me
Richard Whiteley

Catch phrases
(mostly from
Yorkshire Comedians)

It's being so cheerful 'at keeps
me going

The day war broke out, my missus
said to me   *Albert Maddy*

Give 'im the money Barney

Ah'm proper poorly

Ah thowt "right monkey"

There's only them as knows their
own knows

Can I do you now sir?

Ave a go Joe

Ah won't tek mi coat off. Ah'm
not stoppin'

Cheer Up!
(The conslations of
Yorkshire philosophy)

To thi mind – peace
To thi heart – joy
To thi soul – strength
And courage, doy
May thi outgoings
Be nowt amiss
And thi home comings
Happiness

Mi father died at Wibsey tide
An left me all his riches:
A paper cap, a wooden 'at,
a pair of leather britches,
A teapot wi'aht a spaht, a cup
wi'aht a 'annel,
A bacca box wi'aht a lid, an; awf
a tallaw cannel

CATCH PHRASES
TTFN – Ta Ta for Now

Have a smoke o'your own if it's
only as thin as a rat tail

It's better ner a slap int'face wi a
wet haddock

A chap wi' peg legs nivver suffers
wi' corns
It's 'ard what poor fowk mun put
up wi
What insults and snubs they've
to tek
Yet what little is to be expected
If a chap's a black coit on 'is back
As if cloos med a chap any better
Or good shooes improved a man's
heart
As if muck in a suit smelled sweeter
Ner t'same muck wod smell in a cart.
Walter Hampson

Troubles as don't come are always
worse than t'misfortunes we 'av
to face

Things is nivver as black as yar

Nellie's doorstep

Tha'll clog ageen

Tek hod o' thissen

Mek t'best on't

Better than a poke in the eye with
a sharp stick / a frozen mackerel

We're gradily weel off after all
John Hartley

'Av a spell o' laikin

Class

As common as muck / as cheap
as muck

If tha 'as nowt tha 'art nowt,
If tha'd 'ad owt tha'd a been
summat

Plenty blood but no suet

More pull than a canal horse

She reckons she's Lady Muck

Ah'm a member of the multitude
who labour   *John Hartley*

Ee'll only get to t'top o' t'ladder
if 'is dad 'olds it up for 'im

Ee's a self-made man 'as worships
'is creator

She's as common as a door sneck
wi no 'andles

Oo's ee when ee's at 'ome

Crafty

As leet geen as a posser head

As leet geen as a lodging house cat

Crooked bi nature is nivver made
straight bi eddication
An ounce o' mother-wit is worth
a pound o' clergy

Save your breath to cool your porridge

As straight as a woolworker's hook

Ee dropped out of Sunday School

Shake a bridle ower a Yorkshireman an' ee'll get up and steel t'horse

As crooked as a thirty bob note

That crooked ee dunt lie straight i' bed

Ee's one move ahead of t'bailiff

Straight as a dog's 'ind leg

Daft

Mad as a two bob watch

Tuppence short of a shillin'

Ther's nowt under 'is flat 'at

Daftness nivver built owt worth leaving up

As daft as a dish claht

If fowk weren't moastly fooils advertisers would starve
Ten pence t' t'shilling

Tha's not as daft as tha looks

As daft as a brush

A fooil's tongue is long enough to cut 'is own throit

Great clart 'ead

If tha brains were leather tha'd 'ave no shoes

Durst'o think we're med o'toffee

He's only got one oar in the water

Her lid's on too tight

Too daft to come in out o't'rain

Soft in t'ead

'Ee ladles water in a cullinder

As deep as t'Leeds-Liverpool canal

Ee don't play wi a full deck

'Ee's got bats in 'is belfry

Ten chips short of a pennorth

Some's born daft an' some 'as to work at it

Almost as daft as ee looks

Yer great dollop

Yer great cawf-ead

Slack set up

Funny as a fart in a bottle

'Is shuttle int' threaded

DAFT
Ther's nowt under 'is flat 'at

Ee's not got all 'is gubbins

As gaumless as a gooise

As sackless as a booat-'oss

Tha's a barm-pot

Daft as a pay cloise

Three sheets t't'wind

If it was raining soup
he'd be stuck wi' a fork

Her mother dropped a few stitches
when she knit 'er

Lame in t'brain

Ee wor gotten i' slack watter

As daft as a scuttle

Daft as Joe Bloggs dog 'at
jumped in t'river to get out o'
t'rain

My head will never save my feet

'Is lift doesn't go all the way to
the top storey

'Is lift doesn't stop at all floors

Ee's two sandwiches short of
a picnic

If brains were lard he wouldn't
grease a pan

Two bricks short of a pallet

His driveway doesn't go all the way
to the road / to the garage

He needs his attic rewired

He couldn't get a job as t'village
idiot

His belt doesn't go through all
t'loops

His receiver is off the 'ook

His stairs don't go all the way to
the top

Nutty as a fruitcake with the fruit
left out

Tha's got more boots ner brains

As cracked as a pot

Death

Dead as a door nail

As dead as a coffin nail

As dead as a hammer

Pop / cock yer clogs

His clapper's still, his trap is shut,
He says nowt, false nor clever,
He's no more use, nor mischief, but
His ear's to t'grahnd as ever!
James Gregson –
'Epitaph on a Politician'

DESCRIPTIONS
He's got Brewer's Droop

She's in her pine overcoat

Descriptions

Slicker than hen poop on a pump handle

Flashy as a rat with a gold tooth

As fit as a fiddle

As deaf as a yat stowp

As deaf as a haddock

As 'ard as nails

He's got Brewer's Droop

As white as a ghooast

Ee waters t'lawn with beer so it comes up half cut

She's as changeable as t'weather

Not as green as it's cabbage-looking

So crooked he could hide behind
a spiral staircase

His een stood aht like chapel
'at-pegs

He's so crooked, when he dies
they'll have to screw him into
the ground

Ee's reet well balanced wi' a chip
on each shoulder

As bold as brass

Nobbut just a man
Ee's an auld misery guts

As fit as a lop

As leet as a cleg

As wick as a mop

As braan as a berry

Fame is a lump o' nowt inside
a bubble

As busy as a cobbler's Monday

As thrang as a woman's tongue

As sick as a dog

As greedy as a fox in an 'en 'ouse

Stood like a stoup

As good natured as a pump

As sticky as glue

As strong as an 'orse

As long as t'parson's coat

As right as a trivet

As wet as a mill wheel

Ee keeps all 'is chairs at home

Wouldn't say boo to a goose

Short an' sweet like a donkey's trot

Talking to him is like pissing int'
t'wind and trying not to get wet

He's so thin he has to stand in the
same place twice, just to make
a good shadow

Ee's enough to make a saint swear

Ee's that weak 'ee couldn't pull
the skin off a rice puddin'

Cunning as a Barnsley dog

A wooden church, a wooden steeple
Rascally place, and rascally people

Mutton done up to look like lamb

Mucky as a miner's arm pit

That bow legged as couldn't stop
a pig in a snicket

Got a belly on 'im like a breeve's
goit

DUSTBIN (aka Miscellaneous Sayings)
What's for tea besides nowt?

Dim

As grey as a mowdiwarp [mole]

Ee's not the sharpest knife in the drawer

'Is brain's in 'is clogs

As thick as two short planks

Ee want there when brains were handed out

Ee's nobbut a gil in a pint glass

At back of t'queue for brains

For brains he's on t'minimum wage

As dim as a Toc H camp

Dim brains often go wi' nasty tongues

Tha can always tell a Lancastrian. But not much

Ee's a barge wi'out a rudder

EXERCISE
Ah'm fair knackered

Dirt	**Dustbin (aka Miscellaneous Sayings, Perceptions and Yorkshireisms)**
As nesh as us netty	
Ee stinks like a pow-cat / pig / cow clap	I had one of them but the wheel fell off
As mucky as oor beck	Rarer than hen's teeth
A bit o' dirt nivver 'urt anybody	Dooan't forget t'owd fowks
As mucky as a cow's bum	T'pot calling t'kettle grimy behind
Mucky as a middin	What's for tea besides nowt?

Nawther owt ner nowt

Exclamations

Ee by gum. We 'ad a reet fine do

Ah'll go ter t'top of our stairs.
[Yorkshire houses all had stairs to
cram more houses on less land, to
conserve the beauty of the county
and make more money for
landlords]

'Ells bells an' buckets o' blood

Yer great clatter-can

I'll go to our 'ouse

Ah'm that flummoxed ah don't know
whether I need a shit, shave or 'air cut

Sod this for a game o' sodjers

Well ah nivver. Did yer ivver

That's peed on't' chips
[When Grimsby was a fishing port,
Grimsby Town fans would chant
"We've peed on your fish"]

More bollocks ner a herd o'
bullocks

Ah'm blowed

Ah'll gi'e thi what fo'

Ah'm furious fit to burst

Exercise

Fair puffed

Fair payed

Ee's allus up at sparrow fart

Fair knackered

Exhortations

Gerronwiit

Giusabit

Giusummat

Giusago

Giusbestovorder

Gerrout

Except Ye Repent Ye's addit

Goonwi'yer

Gerrintloony bin

Family

Their cat ran through our back yard

She's marrer tiv 'er dad
[East Riding – looks like her
father]

Only them as knows their
own, knows

There's nowt war ner kids.
Only more kids

Fidget

Thar't in an' out like a dog at a fair

As fidgety as a fly in a bottle

Buzzing about like a blue-arsed fly

Up and down like a toilet seat at
Bowling Tide

Up and down like a whore's
drawers

Like a flea on a fairy

Foibles

Ah unbethowt missen

As sour as a crab apple

Ah'd as life lig in bed

Ah'm fast for a bit o' band

Tha jars mi lugs

More chips ner 'Arry Ramsden

Them as sez they dun't like flattery
is fishin' for it

Folk wisdom

If a bairn's teeath's odd,
It'll seean gan ti God

A chap wi bad habits is called
a good fellow

It's easier to find a fault ner to
lose one

When a chap goes t' t'church ee's
nivver short o' company

Fettle t'machine like it war thine

Men flatter thersens. Women like
ter be flattered

As soon as a chap loves peace
better ner ee loves truth there's an
end to 'is usefulness

To a man 'at as wisdom folly is
a relish

A wise man's ignorant o' things not
worth knowing

The things yer see when you 'avn't
got yer gun

Nowt more generous ner boxers.
Whenivver two on 'em meets
each one tries to gie t''other more
ner ee gets

Chop thi own wood an' it'll warm
thi twice

FOLK WISDOM
T'shoemaker's missus and t'smith's mare are allus worst shod

We get what we deserve but only them at t'top admit it

T'shoemaker's missus an' t'smith's mare are allus worst shod

A good way to stop a chap's mooth is to keep your own shut. *John Hartley*

A chap 'at's liberal wi' t'advice is generally niggardly wi' 'is brass. *John Hartley*

There's some born fooils and there's some mek thersens fooils, an there's some get made fooils on. *John Hartley*

Few chaps believe all they ear sed, even when it's thersen 'at tells t'tale. *John Hartley*

Nivver boast about mekken a good start. It's t'finish 'at tells t'tale. *John Hartley*

When tha admits tha wor wrong yesterday tha's wiser today

Trying to look big meks thi small

Good sense is like a stream –
t' deeper it is less t'noise

Closed lips an' open een save yer from many a fratch

Ther's noo cement been invented yet as can patch up a broken reputation

Nivver judge a man's worth bi t'length of 'is funeral procession: deeing may ha' been t'best thing ee ivver did. *John Hartley*

Dooan't think at because yo're one o'd't'rising generations as yer can luk dahn on them as lived befoor. Ya may a'ris'n but yer may 'av started very low down. *John Hartley.*

What a chap gains bi study an' perseverance he aft pays doubly for bi 'is naybors' envy. *John Hartley*

Don't envy a feller because is dad 'as made 'im rich   *John Hartley*

It's easier to find fault wi a chap for what ee's done, ner it is to show 'im ow ee should ha done it. *John Hartley*

Mek t'most o'thissen. It's all tha's got

A chap may change 'is cloos but ee doesn't change issen. A gooise moults every year but it nivver becomes a swan. *John Hartley*

Life wi'aht fire is like summer wi'aht sun

Fowk are quicker to envy your success ner to pity your misfortune

The road to hell is paved wi' good intentions

If a chap could find a contented woman, a chap 'at nivver grumbles, a poet 'at's grown rich bi' 'is pen, a spendthrift 'at isn't in debt, a bonny lass 'at doesn't know it, an' a lad 'at isn't wiser than his fayther, he could start a museum

I believe it is to be wiser to believe in things 'at you cannot comprehend, ner to doubt all 'at yo' connot prove to be true

Best place for a picnic is allus further on

Shew me thi mates an' I'll tell thi' what thou art

Bi friendly to all but familiar wi' few

Fat sorrow is better na' lean sorrow

Worry is like a rocking horse: it gets thi nowhere

Fanned fire, and forced liver, nivver did well yet

A quiet conscience sleeps i' thunder

What is getten over t'devil's back is spent under 'is belly

It's adversity 'at brings prosperity. It's havin' to feight 'at produces pluck. This world is a big battle-field. It makes thi' idle buckle to – th' modest becomes brave, an' th' upright win at th' finish. Snivvelin' will nivver equal strivin'

A turn well done is soon done

Friendship that flames goes out like a flash

A wild goose ne'er laid a tame egg

To give some fowk too much help meks 'em 'elpless

Wilful waste brings woeful want

Friendship increases on visiting friends, but not if tha visits 'em too often

A black hen u'll lay a white egg

A chap wi' a new gold watch allus worries what time it is

It teks two ter fratch an' one to stop it

Politicians study wot 'as bin ter condemn it, what is ter upset it, and t'future for what they can get owt of it

If tha's puff to spare put it by, tha's need it on thi death bed

T'truth nivver 'urt anyone

Fine words butter no parsnips

A watched kettle nivver boils

Nivver prophesy unless tha knows
John Hartley

Food

Eat like a Yorkshireman

There's nowt so quickly forgotten
as meat an' drink

After t'cheese comes nowt

Wait-and-see pudding [said by
the
cook to inquiring children]

Masticate to a pulp

Ah'm 'ungry as a dog

Good

Ee's no July Barber
[not a fly-by-night]

A pocketful o' money an' a cellar
full o'beer

That's reet gradely

Honest as t'day is long

Selling like spice

Ah get crankier an' wicker
ivvery day

Gerronwi'it

Put some lead in thi pencil

As nimble as a bookie's runner

Get agate

Get fettled

Shift thissen

Frame thissen

Get thi brat on and ger agate

Only a bad workman quarrels
with 'is tools

Hackle thissen up

Gormless

Feckless folk are allus fain o' one
another's company

Ee's like t'yeller line. Allus
int'road

Ee's a clunterlugs [someone who
keeps dropping things]

A reet clunter-head

Ee can't see for lookin'
Bladder
[can't do things in the right way]

Blether-'eead [empty head]

Ee'd be late for 'is own funeral

GREETINGS
Weer to bahn?

Gossip

Fain to be wick [glad to be alive]

Use tha brain more than tha wags
thi tongue

Them as thinks t'least tawks
t'most

Sh'telled t'tale from t'thread ter
t'needle

Ee talks an' says nowt, an' ee's
said nowt when ee's done

Knowing what tha says is better
ner saying what tha knows

Greetings

Weer to bahn?

Ah didn't awn yer

Nah then thee. 'Ow arta [Hello]

Ger out o' mi' road

Hopeless

As rare as rockin' 'orse droppins

Ee nivver lets 'is tea mash

God 'elp t'poor cow

Ee gi' us a ton o'nutty slack

He looks like summat that war sent for and didn't come

Her light's on, but there's nobody home

As weak as chip 'oil vinegar

Ee'll be a man afore 'is mother

Ee brought 'is pigs to a free market

Ee couldn't organise a piss up in a brewery

Hunger

It's thi stomach 'at 'ods thi back up

Tha can't work wi'owt packing

Him 'at's etten more than he gradely should is awther greedy or empty

My belly thinks my throit's cut

'Unger's t'best sauce

Mi belly button's knockin' against mi backbone

Ah can eat two potatoes more ner a pig

'Is een are bigger ner is belly

Ah'd eet t'oven door if it were buttered

Illness

As ill as sooit an wesh

Lookin' a bit yonderly

Don't fret thissen

As ill as Owd Nick

Ah've got bellywak

As sick as Richard Whiteley's ferret

You look like death warmed up

'Is breakfast came back to see 'im

Insults

Yer great gobslatch.

Tha's a reet daft-ead / a reet toss pot / reet tosser

He's nowt a pound, an' bumpin' weight at that

Daft as a post / a brick / a stoop

ILLNESS (including teeth!)
Don't fret thissen

IQ (Low, Medium and Yorkshire)
If 'is brains wor dynamite they'd not blow 'is cap off

He's only t'height of three
pennoth o' copper

Tha'r't a parrot-faced wazzock

IQ
(Low, Medium and Yorkshire)

For brains ee's baht

Lame int'brain

If 'is brains wor dynamite they'd
not blow 'is cap off

Limp under t'cap

Kids

Childer suck their mother when
they're young, an' their fayther
when they're grown up.

A child an' a chicken is allus
pickin'

It's easy to bury other folks'
bairns

Nowt's gotten bi chance save kids

Know-alls

He's all talk an' says nowt

Too big for 'is booits / clogs

She's allus callin' an' tootin

Some tawk becoss they think
they're born wi such a lot o' wit,
Some seem to tawk to let fowk
know they're born wi'owt a bit,
Some tawk in 'opes as what they say
may 'elp ther feller men,
But t'moast 'at trawk just tawk
because they like to hear thersen

Know-nowts

If tha wants thi opinions respected
keep 'em to yerssen

When a chap's nowther rich nor
useful ee owt t'get wed. Somebody
mun look after 'im.

Hod thi noise. If tha cannot tawke
some sense keep tha mouth shut
John Hartley

If tha wants ter believe all tha says
say nowt

Lawyers

Fools an' obstinate buggers make
lawyers rich

If you want to be poor goo to law.
Win or lose, it maks varry little
difference

Justice is blind but she in't deaf,
an' 'im 'at can jingle t'moast brass
oft wins t'case.

37

A case in't cellar's worth two in't court

Ee lies like a lawyer

Lawyers are t'only fowk who can work in sewers but nivver stink

Lazy

As idle as a Ludlam dog at leans its 'ead agint wall ter bark

Ees that idle ee thinks manual Labour's a Spanish socialist

Likes work so much he could sit and watch it all day

There's more work in an asprin

As lazy as a ladder at leans agin t'wall
Ee'll only turn ower t'garden in 'is mind

Lies

As big a lier as Tom Pepper an' he were pawsed aht o'hell three times
afore breakfast for lying

He lies like a dirty rug

Liar, liar, pants on fire

Ee's nivver been introduced ter t'truth

Lonely

Ee's a pot o' one
[solitary, withdrawn, independent]

I couldn't warm to thee if we were cremated together

As lonely as a milestone

Ee only likes 'is own company

Meanness

Ee's got short arms and long pockets when it comes ter paying

A deal o' fowk gooa regular to a place a worship but if some on 'em only gets as much religion as they pay for, ah'm feared it in't much   *Ben Preston*

Ee chucks is brass around like a man baht arms

As graspin' as a toll bar

As tight as a damp clothes line

As mean as a cat wi a mouse

T'chap at boasts ee owes nowt to nabdy won't be 'appy if ee means ee didn't intend to pay owt to anybody   *John Hartley*

Weak tea = watter betwitched and tea begrudged

Ee's that mean eed split a current in two

Ee wouldn't part wi't' drips off 'is nose

Ee's that tight ee won't let 'is teeth chatter when ee freezes.

Ee's that mean ee wouldn't pee on yer if yer war on fire

That mean ee won't give yer t'time o'day

If thou wants ta know t'value of a pound, try an' borrer one

Ee wouldn't tell yer tomorrow wa' Sunday if yer didn't know

Charity begins at home in Yorksher and usually stays there

Keep yer 'and on yer ha-penny

It costs too much and a half

Ee gives a gill for t'price of a pint

There's no pockets i'backless neetgahns

He's lower than a snake's belly

He'd sell an anchor to a drowning man

She's so tight she'd squeeze a penny until the queen cried

He's so mean, he wouldn't give you t'drips off his nose

Ee wouldn't part wi't'reek of 'is own muck

Misery and misanthropy

Come back again when tha' can't stay so long
We wipe t'sweat off us brow wi t'slack of us bellies

Nivver do nowt for noabody

Ah reckon nowt to it

As mawngy as an owd cat

As solemn as a coo

Things are that bad even them as nivver pays in't buying

Moods and states

Ah'm sad flayed [I'm scared]

Ah'm fair capped

Bloss up   [Brighten up]

Tha mun gan a dee
[Go away or drop dead]

As dry as a booan

As blind as a bat

39

As thick as inkle weyvers
[narrow tape worm or narrow
loom]

As greedy as a rake

As snug as a bug in a rug

As fat as a mowdiwarp [mole]

As edgy as a crocodile in
a handbag factory

As deaf as a pooast

As waik as a kittling

Mardy as a cat

On mi' beam ends

A pot o' oil [withdrawn; aloof]

Ah'm reet mawky [looking
sickly]

Doan't let's get narky
[bad-tempered, sarcastic]

Up Dicky's meadow
[in difficulties]

Muck

Mucky as a duck puddle

As sure as a louse in Pomfret

Weer there's muck there's brass

As mucky as a pig sty

She's wedded t' t'midden for sake
of t'muck

Tha's like 'orse muck, allus in't road

Ee's allus in 'is muck

Mucky as a midden

Mum
(sayings mi mam sed to us)

Patience is a virtue. Find it where
you can. Seldom in a woman and
nivver in a man

You make a better door than
a window

Tell the truth and shame the Devil

Better to be ten minutes late in
this world than ten years early
in the next

Hard work never hurt anyone

Little birds in their nests agree
[we never did]

How much did you pay for it?
"Money and fair words"

Idleness is nothing unless it's well
followed

Don't be backward in coming
forward

MUCK
Like 'orse muck – allus in t'road

Handsome is as handsome does

Naughty

Tha's marrer to Bonny
[ie Bad as Napoleon]

Tha's war ner our Kate

As straight as a shopping trolley

As cunning as a cart load o'
monkeys

Old Age

There's many a good tune played
on an old fiddle
At seventeen a feller thinks hissen
a clever man
At twenty-five ee knows ee's got
a world reforming plan
At forty ee admits ee didn't larn
soo much at schooil
At sixty he's just larnt enough to
knaw ee's bin a fooil
Walter Hampson

41

An old nowt will nivver be owt

Them at's same age as me is allus
older

I'm as old as my tongue and a
little
older than my teeth

There may be snow on the roof,
but there's still fire in the furnace

Age is when tha needs a rest
afore bed

A new broom sweeps clean but
an old 'un knows t'corners

As old as Methusalah an' twice
as dead

Some folk only behave thersens
when they're too old to do owt
else

Optimism
(a rare virtue)

A breet smile drives away a deep
shadow

Ah'm reet champion

Ah'm reet grand

Mi whippet can give a rabbit three
times round t'cellar an' cop it easy

Overworked

Ah'm reet thrang

As throng as Throp's wife when
she hanged hersen wi t'dish claht

Up to 'er een i'work

Ah'm working an tewin fr' morn
to neet

Perseverance

Keep t'band in't nick

Allus hod on

Hod thi whist

Nivver say nivver

Nivver say nay

Nivver say nowt

Pessimism
(a conditioned reflex)

Old Abe's pig didn't weigh as
much as ee expected it would. An'
ee allus thowt it wouldn't
Walter Hampson

Gie nowt for owt

Yer nivver know oo yer friends are

Nice view but it weant pay t'rent

Ah've been / seen wahr

Nobbut middlin'

Can't say owt's up
[but ah would if ah could]

Mustn't / Can't grumble [ditto]

Philosophy

If it wearn't for summat there'd
be nowt

Summat's better ner nowt

If a man thinks ee's well off ee's
well off

Angels nivver av whiskers

This an' better might do, but this
an'
worse 'll nivver do
Awlus be at t'foor end of a feast an'
t'latter end of a fight

One tale's good 'till another's told

Cop t'lot an' stick [motto of the
Yorkshire Altruism Society]

Pudden's pudden
[Italian Che sera sera]

There's nowt gotten in an 'urry but
chance brats

You can't grow grass on a busy
street

After three days both fish and
guests start to stink

There's more ways ner one to skin
a cat

Maggie, tha'rt bonny,
As bonny as onny;
Mi sovereigns are few
An' mi maisters are monny;
But whahle Ah can weyve,
An' whahle tha can spin,
Well keep trouble aht,
An' happiness in.
William Beaumont

Everyone reaps as ee sows except
ont'allotment

A bit o' help is worth a deal o' pity
A weddin', a woo,
a clog an' a shoe,
A pot full o' porridge
an' away they go

Good folk are scarce, tek care on 'em

Go a borrowin', go a sorrowin'

Tha mun't ever be t'main man at
a weddin' or a funeral

Anyone wi't use of is een can see

PHILOSOPHY

Ther's nowt good bowt cheap

Ther's nowt good bowt cheap

Physical characteristics

As slow as a snail / as a stutterer

As lame as a three-legged dog

As tough as leather

As tall as t'mill chimney

As hoarse as a raven

As wet as t'dish cloot

As soft as putty

As tired as a dog

As full as an egg

Lanky like a cloos prop

A case of brewer's goitre

A belly built int' pub

Places

'Alifax is built of wax
'Eptonstall o' stone
In 'alifax ther's bonny lasses
In 'eptonstall ther's nooan

Said the Devil flyen ower
'arrogate's wells: "Ah think
am 'ome by t'smells"

The muse in Tadcaster can find
no theme
But a most noble bridge without
a stream

The verse before on Tadcaster
was just,
But now great floods we see and
dirt for dust.

Lincoln was, London is, but York
shall be
The greatest city of the three

Oxford for learning, London for wit,
Hull for a woman, and York for a tit

Slowit, weer they raked t'moon
aht o't' watter

Slowit, weer they put t'pigs on
t'wall ter listen t' t'band [also said
of Marsden and Milnsbridge]

Pudsey, weer t'ducks fly backwards,
ter keep t'muck aht o'theer een

Pudsey, weer they've all bald heads
cos they pull 'em aht o' t'pit wi'
suckers

Proud Pudsey, poor people,
High Church and low steeple

Ossett, weer they black-leaded
t'tramlines

When Roseberry Topping wears
a cap,
Let Cleveland then beware a clap
[downpour]

45

Ther's more laikes ner works
i'Barnsla

Bradford for cash,
Halifax for dash,
Wakefield for pride and poverty;
Huddersfield for show,
Sheffield what's low,
Leeds for dirty and vulgarity.

Castleford women must be fair
Cos they wash in both Calder
and Aire

From Hell, Hull and Halifax,
Good Lord Deliver us

When all the world shall be aloft
Then Hallamshire shall be
God's croft

Hutton Rudby, Entrepen
Far more rogues than honest men

Great Kelk where God never dwelt
And honest man never rode
through it

They put a wire fence round Kippax
to keep t'fog aht

Selby was a seaport town
When Goole was but a marsh;
Now Goole it is a seaport town
And Selby fares the worse.

There's Hunt Pot and Hull Pot,
Jingle Pot and Joggle Pot;
A cave without a bottom,
An' another at's deeper still

Wharfe is clear, and Aire is lythe,
Where the Aire drowns one,
Wharfe drowns five

Blood thirsty Dee each year
needs three,
But bonny Don, she needs none

The shelvin', slimy river Don
Each year a daughter or a son.

Ainderby Steeple
Where there are more rogues
Than honest people

Barton for sartin;
Twea churches and nivver a parson

Borrowby Hills an' Newton Broos
Them's t'spos for hosses an' coos.

When Dighton is pull'd down,
Hull shall become a great town

Market Weighton
Robert Leighton;
A brick church
And wooden steeple,
A drunken priest
And a wicked people

Marrick church is seen the best
Just as the sun withdraws to rest

A Scarborough warning:
A word and a blow
But the blow first.
Semerwater rise, Semerwater sink,
And swallow all the town
But this lile house
Where they gave me meat and drink

PLACES – Hutton Rudby
Far more rogues than honest men

Sutton boiled mutton,
Brotherton beef,
Ferrybridge bonny lasses
and Knottingley thief

**Play it down
(Be Yorkshire)**

Summat an' nowt

Nawther mickle nor muckle

More tops ner noils

Owista? Nobbut awfish or Nobbut
nazzard [neither well nor ill]

Better ner yesterday war ner
t'morn

'Appen it is, 'appen it in't

Better ner like [a good day]

That's summat like [OK]

Ah'm nobbut fair ter middlin

Least said soonest mended

Poverty

Friday flits
Have not long sits

If tha wants ter be poor stay
int'pub
John Hartley

He bears poverty ill who's ashamed
on it

Nowt's for nowt

Baht 'owt. Ah'm baht

Ee ant got two ha'pennies for a penny

Ee lives in't' pop shop

Goin dahn t'nick

So poor ee couldn't buy a ticket to a
free lunch

Poverty poverty knock
Mi loom is saying all day
Poverty poverty knock
Gaffer's too skinny to pay
But ah know ah can guttle
When ah 'ear mi shuttle
Go poverty poverty knock
Thos. Sykes Daniel 1889-1970

Tha' clam'd an' hauf damned mi lad,
still tha' t a deal nearer heaven nur
some *John Hartley*

Proverbs

A steady income meks many folk
unsteady

Blessed is t'bride at t'sun shines on
An' blessed is t'dead at t'rain rains on

There's allus t'most thrustin weer
there's t'least room

A dimple in the chin brings
a fortune in
A dimple on the cheek leaves
the fortune to seek

Free advice is only worth its cost

A cobweb i't'kitchen
An feeat marks on t'step
Find noa wood i't'yewn
An' neoa cooals i't'skip

There's nowt like tryin'

T'nearer t'home sweeter t'meeat

Talk o't'devil an' yer'll 'ear is clogs

There's allus room at t'top but
none to sit down

A chap wi' a barrel of ale int'cellar
nivver wants for company

It's a lot better / cheaper / nicer
to live int'past

Life's warp comes throo Heaven,
t'weft's fun bi us sen *John
Hartley*

Queer (all senses)

More camp ner a row o' Boy
Scout tents

Ther's nowt so queer as fowk

As queer as Dick's 'at band

All t'world's queer except thee
and me – and tha's a bit

A real lad-lass
[stolen by Arnold Schwarznegger,
who calls opponents "girly-men"]

Happy as a bugger playing rugger

As queer as a currant bun

**Rag Bag
(a.k.a. Miscellaneous or
Odds an' Sods or
Owt 'at fits nowhere)**

Put t'wood in't oil [My father. In
extreme cases he would shout
"Were you brought up in a barn?"]

Ah'm sad flayed [I'm scared]

Gerrup t'wooden steps to bed
(or climb t'wooden 'ill)

Yan, tean, thethera, methera, pimp
[Ancient Celtic sheep count – not
much used since the Celtic sheep
died off]

Reputation

Have a name to get up early,
an' tha' can lie i'bed all day

Ee's nobbut a gill in a pint pot

Gie a dog a bad name

Sage advice

Say nowt to nobody about nowt
i' no road

Wisdom is ignoring what's not
worth knowing

'Ear all. See all. Say Nowt (Of
course!)

Ate All. Sup all. Pay nowt

Best way to cheer thissen up is to
cheer someone else up

It''s not them 'as knows most
That 'av t'mooast ter say
Nor is it them 'as 'av mooast
That give mooast away

It'll save thi no small trouble
If when speaking tha teks care
Of whom tha speyks to whom
tha speyks
And how and when and where

Get thi brain an' thi' gob inter gear

Tha these them as these thee,
an' tha dunt them as dunt

Temperance means health –
good grub, brass i'th'pocket,
a fair name – happy hooam,
thrivin' bairns – a clear heeard –
an' a breet prospect for hereafter

Better give a shillin' than lend
hafe a craan

Borrowed garments nivver sit weel

Good luck goes to some more than
it should but seldom more than
they want

Give a child while he craves, an'
a dog while 'is tail wags, you'll 'ave
a fair dog, but a poor child

Them 'at never knew pain preach
patience

Neither build thissel up, nor pull
thissel down. If tha builds thissel up
nubdy 'ull believe thee; an' if tha
pulls thissel down, they'll believe
a lot more than tha says

If thou wants a good servant, tek
neither a relation nor a friend

Thou doesn't deserve sweet,
if thou willent taste sour.
Him that does thee an ill turn will
never forgive thee

If when yo're doing yer best, th'
clouds o' misfortun' surround yer,
nivver heed! Keep straight on. Th'
moon shines on, no matter what
clouds obscure it, an' when they've
passed looks breeter nor ever.

A good cow can 'av an ill cawf

A bridle for thee tongue is a
necessary piece o' furniture

Moderation's fine if tha dunt
ower do it

Nivver put a drum set in a
back-to-back

Don't snag [spit] in t'ash trays.
Ah want t'tabs for missen
[sage advice shouted by
Commissionaire at t'bug hole
(a.k.a. Pavilion Cinema), Shipley,
at children's matinées]

If ther's a lot, eat a little.
If there's a little, eat it all

It teks less time to do summat for
folk ner to explain why tha didn't

Them as buys happiness gets
poor value for t'brass

Sayings

If tha Bob dun't gie our Bob t'bob
as thi Bob owes our Bob our
Bob'll
gie tha Bob a bob on't nose

If tha knows nowt say nowt.
If tha knows summat say nowt

Of tools" "It's that sharp tha could
ride bare arsed to Donny on it"

Doan't fash thissen. Tha's got all
t'time there is

Self-sufficiency

If tha wants owt done well,
do it thissen

If tha wants summat interesting,
talk to thissen

If a job's worth doing,
it's worth doing well

If at furst tha don't succeed,
ask thissen why

If at first tha don't succeed,
do summat else

Sex

She's t'town bike

She's showing more meat than
t'butcher's window

Busy as a Hull harlot

Gi'up Gi'ower Gerremoff Gerroff
[South Yorkshire mating call]

Tha's bin tom cattin'

Put 'er t' t'tup

Them as weds weer they don't
love mostly loves weer they don't
wed

Lads love is lassies' delight,
And if lads don't love,
lassies will flite.

Yer don't look at t'mantelpiece
when yer poking t'fire

She lays more ner our 'ens

She goes like a train / tram / steam engine

Ah wouldn't kick 'er out of bed

A bachelor nivver meks t'same mistake once

Single chaps are content wi one woman. Until they get 'er

A chap 'ats allus smilin' an' smirkin' at ivvery woman is soon to be wed

Ee's an awd tup

Sex when tha's old is nobbut tatty watter

As wick as a weasel, kittling, lop, etc

Ee's got summat under 'is brat

Tha'll nivver miss a slice off a cut cake

No 'arm in another spoonful once t'lid's off

She's up t'spout / got a bun in't'oven

Show-offs

Ther's many a showy gown covers a mucky shift

We're all Adam's children, but silks an' satins maks the difference

Better go to heaven i'rags ner to hell i'embroidery

She thinks she's summat but she's nowt

As toff as owd 'Arry

All mouth and trousers

Ee's a reet mee maw (mee mo) [person with affected behaviour]

Shut Up

Od thi wisht

Od thi din

Shut thi cake oil / gob

If silence is golden tha's banked

Giusbestovorder: Shurrup

Stupid
(including Southerners)

Tha talks like an 'alfpenny book baht leaves

Tha knows little an' does less

THUMPS

Ah'll clip thi lugs

It's easier to convince a
philosopher ner it is to win an
argument wi' a fooil *John Hartley*

'Is 'ead'll nivver save 'is legs

Ee asn't enough sense to come in
out of t'rain

As gaumless as a lot o' throttled
earwigs

It's a sackless fooil at's allus
grinning *John Hartley*

Ee's leet weight, on nowt a pund

You can tell fowks from 'Arrogate
but you can't tell 'em much

Tha's a speed bump on the
information highway

He was toilet-trained at gunpoint

Stupid as the day's long

So stupid, when you say 'ello,
ee's stuck for an answer

53

If brains were vinegar she couldn't have enough to pickle an egg

As dim as a Toc H lamp

She's not got every pan on t'oven

Thumps

Fighting like ferrets in a sack

Fratchin's better ner feytin

Sh' fotched 'im a claht

Twelt	}	
Thrash	}	
Fetch 'im one	}	To hit
Flay	}	(Prohibited
Bray	}	for children
Thump	}	up to 45)
Wallop	}	
Hammer	}	

I'll wall thi 'een up

Ah'll clip thi lugs

Reet poshing

Ah'll belt thi into t'middle of next week

Gie 'im a bunch o' fives

Tits

Does ta want a medal or a chest to pin it on?

As flat as a witch's tit

Get yer tits out for t'lads

Yer don't get many of them to a pound

As flat as a yard o' pump watter (Not Jordan)

Toasts

'Eer's to me an' mi wife's 'usband, not forgetten missen

Eer's ti us. May we nivver want for owt. None on us all on us. Ner me neither

The Lord be thanked for what we're getting, If ther'd been more to ate ther'd 'ave been more etten

Them as ates t'most puddin gets t'most meat

God bless us all an mek us able Ter ate all t'stuff 'ats on this table

Mek a lang airm. To a guest at a meal, help yourself and no asking

Fear God. Honour t'King, eat the
porridge an 'od thi din
Here's tae thee and thine
Nat forgettin me and mine
When thee and thine meet
me and mine
May me and mine be as good
to thee and thine
As thee and thine's been to me
and mine

'Ear all see all say nowt
Ate all sup all pay nowt
An if tha 'ivver does owt for nowt
Do it for thissen

Nah cum mi lad, fill up thi glass
We'll drink t'Yorkshire great
in brass
Happier wi every passing year
T'brass gets less but t'great's
still there

From witches an' wizards an'
long-tailed buzzards an' crazy
things that run in hedge bottoms,
Good Lord deliver us.

Trust no one

Phony as a nineteen bob note

He'd steal owt but a red-hot stove

Them as gives nowt gets nowt

Ah'd trust 'im as far as ah could
throw 'im

Ugly

She can't 'elp being ugly but she
could 'av stayed at 'ome

She looks as if she tossed a sparer
an' lost

Ee's a face like a busted clog

She's got one eye on't pot an'
another on't chimney

As plain as a pikestaff

Ee in't bald – ee's shorter ner is 'air

Glasses like pop bottle bottoms

A face like t'back end of a bus

An 'ead like a set pot

As bald as a blether o'lard

Bat-lugs

Four-eyes

As thin as a lat

Ah've seen better 'air on bacon

Smiling like a cracked piss pot

Got a grin like a butcher's dog

A smile like a wave in a slop pail

Red as a spanked baby's bum

She fell in't rag bag and got out dressed

He's got friendly eyes: they're allus lookin' at each other

When t'wind changes tha'll stay like that

She's as pretty as a bald-faced heifer

Seen more 'air on a coconut

She's a used car with a new paint job

He's so ugly that when he was born the doctor slapped his mother

She was so ugly she got a job as a test pilot in a broom factory

All fur coat an' no knickers

Untidy

Ah'm in mi'muck

Ah've got 'ands that feel like Dick's feet

All over t'shop

Tidy as a tip

Neat as a netty

Useless

Tha' mind's like a shop: no use if it's closed

As much use as a chocolate fireguard

Tha can educate some folk till they're daft

As handy as a duck wi a muck fork

All tha' gets from a pig is t'grunt

As useless as a man made o' band

Ee couldn't 'it t'barn door sat ont' sneck

As useless as a chocolate teapot

As much use as casters on a crutch

Useless as tits on a bull

As much use as a pocket in a shroud

Tha great clod hopper

Tha's a waste o' space

Useless as a ten bob watch

Wealth

Better go to heaven i'rags, noer to 'ell i'embroidery

UGLY

Seen more 'air on a coconut

USELESS
Tha great clod hopper

It int wat tha 'as as meks yer 'appy
but things yer doan't as meks yer
miserable

Them as 'as, gets

It's nobbut three generations from
clogs to clogs

A chap wi' a metal watch is nivver
feared o'pick-pockets

Ee 'as brass comin' out o' 'is ears

Charity begins at 'ome i'Yorkshire
and usually stays there

Weather

For every fog i'March, there'll be
a frost i'May

Deean't cast a cloot
Till May bi oot

Ya moan't wesh blankets i' May,
Or else ya'll wash yer soul away

Happy is the bride the sun shines on
Blessed is the corpse the rain falls on

I see t'mean an' t'mean sees me
God bless t'sailors oot on t'sea

Onion skin
Very thin
Mild weather coming in:
Onion skin thick and tough
Coming winter cold and rough

The first cock of hay
Frights the cuckoo away

It's silin i'stair rods

It's goin ter sile it down

It wor sleetin' bad enough to tek
pleasure out of a buryin'

If the cock crows going to bed
He'll certainly rise with a watery
head

As cold as Christmas

If it rains 'afore seven,
it'll be fine 'afore eleven

A peck o'March dust, an' a
shower i'May, makes corn green,
an' t'fields gay

The east wind is too lazy to blow
round you, it goes straight through

A mackerel sky not varry long wet
not varry long dry

A green Christmas maks a fat
churchyard

More raan, more rust

It's looking black over our Will's
Mother's [it's going to rain]

Ossin ter slart [it's starting to rain]

If tha dunt like us weather 'ang on.
There'll be some more along

WEATHER
I'Eptonstall when t'wind snaps they all fall over

That cold folk 'ave their 'ands
in their own pockets

Raan raan faster
T'bull's int'pasture
Raan raan go away
Cum agaan another day

I'Eptonstall when t'wind snaps
they all fall ower

Fine weather's not allus t'best

Wed
(and other states of misery,
not including Gay
partnerships or livin' ower
t'brush – or ower t'latch)

When everything goas wrong wi'
a chap an' ee cannot lay t'blame
on 'is wife 'is marriage is a failure

When a cook gets wed she's
nivver any dripping for sale

Livin' tally, ower t'brush

A ring round yer fingers is worth
two round yer een

Nivver put yer 'usband on a pedestal,
'Eel nobbut want dustin'

It's a good horse at nivver
stumbles,
an' a good wife as nivver grumbles

Hot tongue and cold shoulder for
tea

Faults are thick where luv is thin

When a plain woman weds she dunt
invite 'er beautiful sister to live

Tha needs a wife or an allotment

Many a rich bachelor meks a poor
'usband

Nivver luv brass but allus luv weer
brass is

Marry in Lent
Tha'll live to repent

More belongs to marriage than
four bare legs in a bed

Lasses want nowt but husbands,
an' when they 'ave 'em, they want
ivverything

A chap cannot thrive who 'as
a wasteful wife

It's not every couple as meks a pair
Every lass can keep house better
than her mother, 'til she tries

When poverty comes in through
t'door, love flys out 'at winder

There's more gets wed na does well

Sam Smith's livin' wi a
single woman
Ee couldn't find a double woman
'at ud 'av 'im

Afore they're wed ee can't live
baht 'er. After ee can't live wi 'er

When tha wife's quiet nivver ask
'er ter do owt – she's enuff ter do to
put up wi' thee

**Women
(also incoporating bags, bints,
birds, slags, slappers, slatterns,
slovens, sluts, talent, tarts,
trollops and tosspots)**

Only one thing's more changeable
ner a woman an' that's two

A woman o' thirty sez she's twenty-
five but when she's sixty she'll
boast o' seventy

She's allus chewing t'bacon

Single chaps are content wi' one
woman. Until they get 'er

As flat as a yard o' pump watter
Ya cannot mak' ale wi'out watter
Nor Yorksher Pud baht batter
But a feller needs nowt t'mek
trouble an' strife
If ee lives wi 'is mother-in-law
an' 'is wife *Walter Hampson*

Gie a woman an inch an' she
reckons she's a ruler

Be wary be chary
Tek heed who tha courts
Ther's lasses i'plenty
I'sahzes n' sorts.
But if tha's be happy
Tek on wi a lass
At's nimble wi't' thimble
An' careful wi't brass.
*Rhymes in the North Country
Humour,* 1971

Sympathy's what tha' mun give
a woman to get t'full story

Never tell a Yorksher lass tha's
not worthy on 'er
Let 'er find out for 'ersen

She's allus chewin' t'cud

What should a lass learn afoor
getting wed? Learn to play
t'pianner or ha to mek a dress; but
learn to mek a pie first. That's
t'promise to keep *John Hartley*

Nivver blame a lass for spending
'er brass on a stylish bonnet. It
may be a means o' grace. She's
pretty sewer to attend t'chapel

regular for a Sunday or two
John Hartley

A bonny young lass is varry charmin'
but a nice old woman is still
sweeter an' more soul satisfyin'

A dog's nose and a maid's knees
are allus cowld

If time ivver comes when all men
are brothers, then all th' wimmin
will be sisters, an' that'll be
awkward

Women are a disagreeable lot.
When two on em fall aht, which
ever comes to tell you abaht it,
it's allus t'other one to blame
Walter Hampson

Ter mek 'omes dearer
An' dark skies clearer
An' bring 'eaven nearer
Is women's work *John Hartley*

If tha's looking for a perfect
woman, gi' ower. She's deead.

Ther's nowt meks a woman as mad
as 'aving a saycret nobody wants
ter know.

A woman's tongue wegs like
a lamb's tail

She'd start a fight in an empty house

She was pure as the snow but she
drifted

She's narrower than hen's eyes

Homely as a row of back-to-backs

Work

Workin' for little is better ner laikin

'Ard work nivver killed anyone /'
'urt anyone / did anyone any 'arm

Twist an' turn, reel an wind
Keep a contented mind

Life's all bed an' work

If tha dunt work tha dunt eat

Nivver heed. It'll come to Saturday

Work's fascinating. Ah can watch
fowk doing it for hours

A collier lad a collier lad
A collier lad for me O
He works in a hole as black as t'coal
And brings all 'is brass 'ome to me O
*West.Riding mining ballad from
A.L. Lloyd, Come all ye bold miners*

There's no time off when tha's
nowt ter do

Mining: A job for life
NCB adverts, 1970

Ah tew on tool all day fer nowt

Better to work ner to fret

Better sit idle ner work for nowt
Ther's t'meat hung dahn afor t'fire
to roast
Ther's t'pudden on t'brondee afore
it ta toast
Potatoes top o't' hop, they'll be done
enif souin
But ah think tha can weave a few
more bobbins bi nooin
*[John Bromley – White Rose
Garland, 1947]*

Work's that good for thi, tha's best
leaving some of it til tomorrow

Working on a dead 'orse
[doing work already paid for]

If ya miln pieces reit
An ya cuttle'em streit
An finish em fit for to wear
Then your wage sud be good
An your work sewerly sud
Not leave ya o'en burdened wi' care
Ben Turner

Nivver grummel becos yer've got to
work: a lazy chap is nivver happy.
John Hartley

If yer could get all yer want for
th' axin for yer'd goa to work for t'
pleasure on it *John Hartley*

'Ard work nivver killed anyone
But t'thowt on it's killed thousands

Nivver buy owt wi' a wooden handle
– it allus means hard work

Gurt tawkers are seldom gurt workers

Gi' us some bulwark   [extra effort]

Tha dunt mek footprints on't'sands
o' time sat on thi bum

**Yorkshire
(including best, biggest, beautiful,
bounteous, brilliant and
bloody good)**

Eat like a Yorkshireman

Don't speak t'Queen's English.
It's t'Queen's Yorksher tha needs

Tha's not from round 'ere

A day can't sooart all a
Yorkshireman
Wun at's was nur sum bud not
much
John Hartley

As Yorkshire as they mek 'em

Yorkshire's hills and moors,
Lancashire's mills n' hoors

Yorkshire watter: too wet to walk
on,
too dry to drink
And allus in short supply

Yorkshire born and Yorkshire
bred.
Strong in t'arm an' thick int' 'ead

If tha can't tawk sense to a
Yorkshireman then say nowt
an' shut thi gob.

An offcumden 'll nivver mek a
Yorkshireman

Shake a bridle ower a
Yorkshireman's grave
an' ee'll rise an steal t'orse

T'END